WATER-COLOURS BY

PAUL CÉZANNE

WITH THIRTY-TWO PLATES IN COLOUR

SELECTED

AND WITH AN INTRODUCTION

BY GEORG SCHMIDT

BRITISH BOOK CENTRE · NEW YORK

1953

TRANSLATION BY GLYN T. HUGHES

PRINTED IN THE NETHERLANDS

COPYRIGHT 1952 BY

HOLBEIN PUBLISHING COMPANY LTD. · BASLE

WHEN we look at the water-colours of Paul Cézanne, our enthusiasm persuades us that we are justified in the unjustifiable gesture of an unqualified judgement. Cézanne's water-colours, we cry, are the most sublime realization of the whole art of water-colour painting.

Similarly we feel tempted to see in Cézanne's drawings the essence of all drawing, in his oil-paintings the essence of all painting in oils. This is a measure of the extent to which Cézanne gives to every tool, every material and every technique all that essentially belongs to that tool, material or technique.

For Cézanne the water-colour is not merely a stage between the drawing and the oil-painting. Certainly it is that too, and, as we shall see, in a particularly subtle way, but at every stage between the first striking of a chord of colour and the fuller orchestration each water-colour has a completeness of its own. And for the later Cézanne the water-colour is in a sense the royal road of painting; his later works in oils increasingly acquire the freedom and transparency of the water-colour.

The water-colour indeed accompanies Cézanne throughout. However, in the early period from 1858–1871, which Venturi* has called the 'academic and romantic period', the more phlegmatic colour of oils is better suited to the artistic purpose. The same also applies, in a lesser degree, to the 'impressionist period' (1872–1877). In the 'constructive period' (1878–1887) the water-colour fulfils its strict function in the development from the drawing to the oil-painting, but in the last, 'synthetic period' (1888–1906), the water-colour more and more takes the lead and gives to the oil-painting something of its liquidity and light. The water-colour is the last and most mature realization of Cézanne's art.

This must not however be taken as implying that the 'constructive' Cézanne does not in himself represent a fulfilment. Indeed for many years it was in this 'constructive' Cézanne that the real Cézanne was seen, and the later figure slipping away into water-colours was taken as a kind of phenomenon of age, leaving critics rather at a loss.

* Lionello Venturi: Cézanne, son art – son œuvre. Paris, Paul Rosenberg, 1936. – 1 vol. text: Catalogue of the works; 1 vol. plates: 1,643 illustrations. With a very full bibliography from 1865–1936 and a list where the works are housed.

For a long time artistic and critical discussion of Cézanne turned exclusively around the 'constructive' period and the question whether Cézanne was, or was not, the 'father of Cubism'. The fact that Cubism sprang from the 'constructive' Cézanne can be denied or depreciated only by someone who applies to artistic paternity the notion, repugnant alike to biology and history, that the father exists only for the sake of the son, instead of, in the first instance, for his own sake.

That in 1908, two years after Cézanne's death, early Cubism kindled its torch at the flame of the 'constructive' Cézanne is a historical fact which does not necessarily have anything to do with Cézanne's own intentions. We have long been able to review the history of Cubism closely enough to know that Cubism merely had its origins in the 'constructive', or, to put it plainly, in the 'cubist' Cézanne, and already from 1910 on Cubism was going its own, to put it equally plainly, increasingly anti-cubist way. Again, it was the beginnings of Cubism relatively closest to Cézanne which, for the sake of the Cubic, excluded the whole broad field of colour, which, for Cézanne himself, was always of cardinal importance. Thus it is equally foolish to attempt to deny Cézanne's paternity in the case of Cubism and to attempt to reduce Cézanne's own importance to the fact of this paternity.

We have also long known however, that about 1912 there arose alongside, and indeed in opposition to Cubism, a movement for which the later Cézanne may equally well be claimed as father: the Orphism of Robert Delaunay, that is to say, permeation by colour.

With the originally undeniably greater historical importance of Cubism the importance of Delaunay was long unrecognised. But whilst Cubism in all its phases – the total cubic (1908–09), the analytical (1910–11), the chromatically neutral flat-pattern (1912–13), and the coloured flat-pattern (1914–24) – has long been a thing of the past, Orphism has experienced a real renaissance in the most recent art. An example of this is the resurrection of Jacques Villon from almost complete oblivion (Villon was born in 1875, that is to say six years before Picasso and ten before Delaunay). It is in the light of the most recent art, and not merely that of France, that we have first really learned to see the later Cézanne, and thus too the particular beauty and especial importance of his late water-colours.

Cézanne was born in 1839. His contemporaries are what one very broadly calls the Impressionists: Pissarro (b.1830), Manet (b.1832), Degas (b.1834), Sisley (b.1839), Monet (b.1840) and Renoir (b.1841). None of these painters has anything like the same actuality for the art of the twentieth century as Cézanne. Their influence has long since reached its term.

How little historical influence should be equated with artistic importance is shown however by Manet, who was indeed at one with the Impressionists in their opposition to official academic art, but who had already found his own artistic fulfilment in the years between 1860 and 1870 (in the decade, therefore, before the Impressionists), and who only associated himself very hesitatingly with Impressionism in its maturity. Manet's 'light-tone Pleinairism' (in contrast to Courbet's 'dark-tone Pleinairism') has had only one important follower: Max Liebermann. And yet Manet himself is one of the really great painters of the nineteenth century. Just as Courbet's great compositions of the Fifties are the authentic portrayal of provincial France, of the village and the small town, Manet's figure pictures of the Sixties are the authentic portrayal of the dweller in the growing big towns.

Renoir, it is true, in his naive joy in colour wherever it is most vivid, followed Impressionism in its universality of colour, that is, in the breaking up of natural light into the elements of the spectrum; but he parted from pure Impressionism in his equally naive joy in the narration of human event, which was for Impressionism almost approaching a sin against the spirit of the fair craft of painting. Renoir had to fashion absolutely plastic bodies. To let the plastic dissolve in the colour-saturated light-filled space, as Monet did, was something Renoir could not find it in his heart to do. On the contrary his bodies became increasingly spherical and thus he parted from the Impressionists as early as about 1880. The necessity for plastic expression even led him to take lightly what was still tabu even for the Impressionists: the correctness of anatomical proportions. Thus the later Renoir participates in the at once anti-Impressionist and anti-academic renaissance of the plastic in the Eighties (Seurat) and, after the basically flat-pattern and basically linear interlude of the Nineties (Toulouse-Lautrec and the Art Nouveau), in the first decade of the twentieth century.

Then finally the relationship of Degas to Impressionism is more distant even than that of Manet. His descent from Ingres and Puvis de Chavannes and his own eminent sensitivity for the plastic and at the same time for the linear enabled him to withstand the temptations of impressionist colourfulness up to the Eighties. Then however in his late pastels the blending of the pronouncedly plastic with mother-of-pearl coloration brought him close to Renoir. His own creative originality however lies in the representational mastery of space. Of the six basic principles of Naturalism – the illusion of space, the illusion of volume, the illusion of the subject matter, the integrity of the drawing detail, the correctness of the proportions and the correctness of the colour of the object – the Impressionists had overcome the following four: the illusion of volume, the illusion of the subject matter, the integrity of the drawing detail and the correctness of the colour of the object. They had retained therefore only the illusion of space and the correctness of the proportions. As colour-saturated space was everything to them, but as they nevertheless at least weakened the space-creating medium of colour perspective by their interweaving of complementary colours (cold green as nearly as possible directly adjoining warm red and cold blue near warm orange), they gave to linear perspective an even greater importance (their predilection for foreshortened streets, rivers and river banks!). In contrast to this Degas led the first attack on linear perspective by shifting the horizon near to the upper edge of the picture and, indeed, beyond it, and thereby making prominent, in the view from above, the surfaces – floors and walls – which delimit space. Increased prominence achieved in this way always means however increasing the flat-pattern pictorial impression. And again, accentuation of spatial depth always means accentuation of the distance between subject and object, whereas abolition of spatial depth means abolition of this distance, that is to say, expressive intensifying of the experience of the object. It is not only in the world from which he draws his subjects – racecourse and ballet – that Degas is the direct forerunner of Toulouse-Lautrec, but equally in his bold, flat-pattern expressive methods of composition.

There remain therefore as pure Impressionists only the three artists: Pissarro, Monet and Sisley.

For Cézanne is, from the first impressionist stroke of the brush which he made in 1872 as a disciple of Pissarro, the most radical anti-Impressionist. And of all the painters of his generation Cézanne met with the most passionate and persistent rejection. Before Cézanne was understood even the other two great surmounters of Impressionism, Gauguin (b.1848) and Van Gogh (b.1853) had had their effect.

After the unproblematical serenity of the Impressionists and their optimistic acceptance of the growth of the large town, an acceptance which owed nothing to the official bombast of the years of the speculators between 1870 and 1890, Europe, in the last decade of the century of industrialisation, sank into a pessimistically backward-glancing, critical, melancholic *fin de siècle* attitude. Cézanne's art, apparently so completely unproblematical from the human point of view, had nothing to say to this; but Gauguin, Van Gogh and the generation of the sixties (Ensor b.1860, Munch b.1863, Toulouse-Lautrec b.1864) had clearly everything to say to it.

This however only explains the indifference of his contemporaries towards Cézanne and not the almost malignant rejection which befell him up to the threshold of old age. Neither is it the case with Cézanne that, as often happens, an originally promising talent was regretfully believed and asserted to have gone astray. The hostility applied to his beginnings at twenty five no less than to his fulfilment at fifty.

The reason for this may be shown with precision.

Having already as a schoolboy at the Lycée of his home-town Aix-en-Provence decided to be a painter, Cézanne took drawing and painting lessons from 1854 on in the town Art School. The outcome pleased the pupil as little as the teacher. According to the standards of a contemporary Art School Cézanne was simply without talent. He took his school-leaving certificate at the end of 1858 only at the second attempt. His father, formerly a hatter and now a banker, decided that the only son (there were two daughters, one two and one five years younger) should study law. The son acquiesced, but got no further than the first preparatory examination. In 1861 with his mother's help his wish to be a painter prevailed with his father, and in April of that year, accompanied it is true by his father and elder sister, he was allowed to go to Paris to attend an academy.

The earliest surviving pictures date from these years 1858–60. Neither technically nor spiritually do they betray a precocious talent – quite otherwise. Measured by the standard of academic-naturalist craftsmanship they are, quite simply, amateurish, and spiritually these late biedermeier genre scenes and landscapes are depressingly fusty and provincial (Venturi Nos. 9–11, 26, 28). In the eyes of his admiring schoolfriends however the young Cézanne was something quite other – an original and self-willed genius, a winged poet (he wrote French and Latin verses), temperamental and indeed passionate. But at the same time over-sensitive, rapidly oscillating between haughty self-assurance and the deepest depressions, between aggressiveness and shyness, sociability and solitude, and at once weak and stern in his decisions. And always extravagantly indulgent towards the weak.

In Paris Cézanne attended the Académie Suisse. This was his first contact with the art capital of the world, in which Ingres was then wielding the sceptre, Delacroix finishing the ceiling of St-Sulpice, and Courbet fighting his noisy battle for realism, and this contact with Paris ended for Cézanne in the bitterest despair. As early as the autumn of 1861 he had to return to Aix, not as a painter, not as a lawyer, but, submitting to his father's wishes, as an employee of the family bank.

8   His emotions however were more than ever in painting. By the end of 1862 his father was forced to admit that, despite the scant encouragement for either party in the results hitherto, his son would either be a painter or nothing. On condition that he sent in his name for the entrance examination to the Ecole des Beaux-Arts his father allowed him to go again to Paris in November 1862.

In the few surviving works of the years 1861–62 Cézanne came not one step closer to his father's academic ideal; on the contrary, having clearly been corrupted at his first visit by Delacroix, Daumier and Courbet, he broke out of the strait-jacket of the polished academic painter of his first works, and, following closely Delacroix's teaching, painted and drew at the same time in bold impasto, and gave to his dammed-up passions their first forceful expression. A small 'Judgement of Paris' (15 cm high by 21 cm broad; Venturi No. 16) is very close to Delacroix.

In external size as well as inner compulsion the chief work of these years is the 'Profile Portrait of his Father reading a Newspaper' (168,5 cm high by 114 cm broad; Venturi No. 25). It was alarming not only for his father, who expected nothing of him, but also for his friends, who expected all. Full of errors (deformities would be a better word!) in anatomy and perspective, it is from the academic point of view hopelessly, even grotesquely untalented, like the early works of Van Gogh. As a human and artistic statement however it has an absolutely brutal reality.

The worst and the best together – already we have here the whole Cézanne. So he will remain to the end, to the magnificent portraits of the gardener Vallier from the last years of his life. Cézanne will never learn to draw correctly in anatomy and perspective, however often he may himself speak of correct linear perspective. In one other respect too this first masterpiece, and a few years later every canvas and sheet of paper to which Cézanne puts his hand, is profoundly contradictory of the self-condemnation which he repeated times without number until his death, namely that his vain endeavour had been for 'realization'. The whole greatness and the whole secret of Cézanne's art lie precisely in the fact that every drawing, every water-colour, every oil painting at whatever outward stage of being finished or unfinished is artistically, that is to say spiritually and sensuously, complete. The notoriously 'unfinished' state of the great majority of Cézanne's works has nothing whatever to do with 'sketchiness'. The sketch is a self-contained artistic act. With Cézanne every sheet and every picture in every phase of its growth is at once an end and a possible new beginning.

Three things together are then the real reason why Cézanne was, of all his genera-tion, the one longest and most passionately opposed, and why the two younger painters, Gauguin and Van Gogh, were understood before him: his constant in-difference towards academic anatomy, towards classical perspective and towards outward finish. It is true that Gauguin disregarded perspective space and Van Gogh anatomical correctness, but both of them at least painted 'finished pictures' – which, in Cézanne's judgement, was the reason for the banal stratification of their pictures. From 1872 on, however, Cézanne's anatomical and perspective de-formities cannot be explained away like Van Gogh's in terms of subjective need for self-expression, but must be understood from an, admittedly no less passionate, objective formal intention, and as for the unfinished nature of all his works, Cé-zanne himself repeatedly confessed to this.

Unmistakably Cézanne though the portrait of his father in 1860–62 is in its inmost nature, it took another ten years before his plough turned new ground in the realm of artistic media as well.

Today we think of Cézanne as the great objective artist, the great antithesis of an art of subjective confession, as the great anti-Expressionist. Cézanne was not that from the very beginning but became it only in ten years of agonised struggle with himself, with a need for self-expression no less extreme than that which afflicted Van Gogh throughout his life. The objectivity and serenity of Cézanne's mature art is the result of a great victory over the temptation of basing his art on the confession of his personal distresses.

After what we have had to say of Cézanne's nature, his family and the provincial milieu of Aix, it is clear that a profound need for self-expression was only too substantially based, at least in the decisive years of development. A point of decisive psychological importance was the relationship with his father, who was never able to forgive his only son for not having been like himself and for being generally regarded in Aix as a crank unfit for normal life. The inferiority complex implanted in him in Aix also embittered for years his relations with women. Not until he was thirty-one did Cézanne establish any profound relationship with a woman. About 1870 he got to know, probably as one of the models, a twenty-year old girl; in January 1872 their only son, Paul, was born. For years however Cézanne found it necessary to resort to the most undignified stratagems to conceal this affair from his father, although, or perhaps because, his father had not legalised his own marriage until five years after the birth of his son. And until 1878, that is to say until he was in his thirty-ninth year, the banker's son had regularly to apply to his friends for money in order to be able to live with his family. Not until 1886, when he was forty-seven, did he legalise his marriage. Half a year later his eighty-eight-year old father died. Cézanne inherited enough to make possible for him from then on a life free from material cares. His way of life however did not change and he remained outwardly completely unpretentious. The only change was that he could now afford more comfortable studios and that, at the early onset of the complaints of old age, he took a cab every day as far as the subject in hand. There remained too above all the strange contradiction between the tranquil continuity and concentration of his work and the continual, almost fugitive, change of domicile in Provence and all around Paris. Yet even in this change one finds his peculiar persistence; for decades Cézanne sought out again and again the subjects which he has made famous: Jas de Bouffan, L'Estaque, Gardanne, Château Noir, Bibémus, the Montagne Sainte-Victoire.

When Cézanne went to Paris for the second time at the end of 1862, he arrived just in time for the famous Salon des Refusés early in 1863. Manet's 'Breakfast on the Grass' made a great impression on him. His emotional state was at the time however nearer the expressive Delacroix than the cool, detached Manet. In February 1864 Cézanne wrote to a young painter friend in Aix that he had been working for months at a copy of a painting by Delacroix. In 1863 Cézanne became acquainted at the Académie Suisse with Pissarro, Monet, Sisley and Renoir. At the beginning of 1864, following his father's wish, Cézanne presented himself for the entrance examination to the Ecole des Beaux-Arts – clearly without success, for in the summer of 1864 he was back in Aix again. By the beginning of 1865 we find him once more in Paris.

There survive from these years 1863–64 three large compositions: after Sebastiano del Piombo ('Christ in Limbo', 170 cm high by 97 cm broad; Venturi No. 84), after Veronese ('The Banquet', because of its uncouth savagery usually called 'Orgy', 130 cm high by 81 cm broad; Venturi No. 92), and after Courbet ('The Bather', 166 cm high by 103 cm broad; Venturi No. 83). The beneficial influence of his concern with Courbet makes itself felt technically as giving sensuous quality to the painting, spiritually in the effort to remain in all his force of expression unromantic and realist, as he had succeeded in doing in the sweep of the 'Profile of my Father reading a Newspaper' of 1861–62.

To these years probably belong also two still-life studies (Venturi Nos. 60 and 63) which, with all their Courbetesque dark-toned impasto, already contain what is most essential in the mature still-life painter, namely indifference to the material

content of the subjects and the powerful rhythmical energy in the concord and
clash of forms (horizontal-vertical, slender-bulging, round-angular, large-small).

In the spring of 1865 Cézanne for the first time sent in work to the Salon and experienced his first rejection. The sensation of the Salon of 1865 was Manet's 'Olympia' painted in 1863. Alien though Cézanne found its technical bravura and its sphinx-like imperturbability it nevertheless persistently engaged his attention, and as late as 1870 he set alongside Manet's dispassionate 'Olympia' his own wildly impassioned 'Modern Olympia'. In the winter of 1865–66 he was working in Aix; from February 1866 on he was again in Paris. Once again he entered for the Salon and was again rejected, in company this time with Manet. His picture, it was said, looked 'as if it had been painted with a pistol'. At this time too he got to know Manet, whom he had admired since 1863. In August 1866 he was again in Aix at his father's country house 'Jas de Bouffan'. The winter of 1866–67 he spent in Paris.

In the years 1865–66 Cézanne had developed from Courbet's spatula technique a language of painting which, pointing beyond the hitherto isolated eruptions of genius, showed itself for the first time capable of sustaining a more continuous production. The result, above all, is the magnificent series of nine portraits of the bearded 'Uncle Dominique' as monk, as advocate, in a turban, in a night-cap (Venturi Nos. 72–77, 79–82). Whilst however it is characteristic of Courbet's spatula technique that it lays on the colour in thin, discontinuous, diaphanous coats, Cézanne builds up the canvas in compact layers as if with a plasterer's trowel. The brush at most retraces a contour. Here already dark spatula surfaces abut angularly and without transition on light ones and thus produce, instead of a continuously rounded, a stereometric corporeality. Of all these portraits that of Uncle Dominique as a Monk (Venturi No. 72) is rightly regarded as the masterpiece. It is like a voluntary confession, or indeed like a self-portrait. Everything serves the warding off of the passions, the monk's cowl, the cross, the arms folded over the breast; and the passions, walled in by heavy spatula layers, blaze inwards.

The application of this spatula technique to landscape (Venturi Nos. 33–38, 46) cannot be as successful since the plein-airist sparkle of the atmosphere in light is ideally suited by Courbet's spatula technique, whereas Cézanne's is inimical to it. Cézanne's spatula rocks, for instance, remain without atmosphere, in the foreground with no impression of space. In their violent chiaroscuro however these landscapes have nevertheless something of the force of expression of the Dominique portraits.

Cézanne's spatula technique of the years 1865–66 is more suited to the still-life, which has no need of space. The 'Skull with Candlestick' (Venturi No. 61) is but little inferior to the Skulls of the late period (Venturi Nos. 758–59) in technical and expressive impetuosity. The still-life 'Loaf and Eggs' (Venturi No. 59) is already characteristically Cézanne in its rhythmical construction – the double horizontals of the loaf cut lengthways, the double verticals of the glass and jug, the two eggs, the two onions, and, for the first time, the double diagonals of the white cloth hanging down from the edge of the table and of a knife laid right across it.

The years 1867–71 mark the eruption, the climax and the close of this expressive early period of Cézanne's. The freely roaming brush breaks through the built-up spatula layers. In all spheres, the figure composition, the portrait, the still-life and the landscape, masterpiece follows masterpiece.

The external circumstances of Cézanne's life now ran their course almost uniformly between Aix and Paris, with continual submissions to the Salon and continual rejections – in 1867, 1868, 1869 and 1870. About 1870 Cézanne got to know Hortense Fiquet (b. 1850). He fled the war to L'Estaque on the Mediterranean coast near Marseilles. In January 1872 his son, Paul, was born. It is undoubtedly correct to connect the end of the expressive early period with this alteration in Cézanne's family affairs. In the spring of 1872 Cézanne was at last ready to enrol in the school of Impressionism with Pissarro.

Amongst the figure compositions of these five years the 'Temptation of St. Anthony' (Venturi No. 103) belongs in time to the beginning. It is the key work to the whole early period. The saint is not tempted by naked and seductive beauty; the four temptresses are of an almost toadlike ugliness. Cézanne veritably rages at the flesh. Of his portraits during this period one of the subjects said that it was as if Cézanne felt that he needed to be revenged for some offence. From the artistic point of view this attitude has two important consequences. One is that the theme is mercilessly removed from the detached sphere of historical convention into the world of psychological reality – St. Anthony is Cézanne himself. The 'Temptation of St. Anthony' is a wholly unromantic, radically realistic work. In contrast the large 'Abduction' dated 1867 (90,5 cm high by 117 cm broad; Venturi No. 101) is still as if 'after Rubens' and the small picture 'Satyrs and Nymphs' (Venturi No. 94) is still as if 'after Titian'. The second result of this attitude is that the completely outrageous deformities turn into form. Grotesquely formless according to the naturalistic conception of what is correct, these breasts, bellies and thighs are optically of the very highest formal power. The equally strongly expressive 'Washing of the Dead' (Venturi No.105) is like a secularised Entombment; it has the inexorable gravity of the late Rembrandt.

The figure compositions of the second part of these five years dispense with historical themes. The 'Modern Olympia' (Venturi No.106) expressly emphasises the renunciation of the historical. It is also admittedly a 'Temptation', but the person led into temptation, sitting in the foreground on the right with his back to us, is a bearded man in modern dress – clearly Cézanne himself. And at the back heavy draperies open revealing a woman cowering toadlike and a naked negress. Once again Cézanne adopted one of the famous compositions of the young Manet, the 'Breakfast on the Grass' (Venturi No. 107) and once again he placed himself, psychologically as the main figure, in the foreground. Here too the greater power of expression is on Cézanne's part. The magnificently grave 'Pastorale' (Venturi No. 104, drawing Venturi No.1208) is like a blending of a 'Temptation' with a 'Breakfast on the Grass'; three nude women on a bare river bank, and lying fully clothed beside them with propped-up head a bearded man – Cézanne himself. Sultry, passionate chiaroscuro.

What dreams haunted Cézanne in these years are shown in such pictures as 'Murder' (Venturi No.121), 'The Strangling' (Venturi No.123), 'The Courtesans' (Venturi No.122) and 'Afternoon in Naples', with a man and woman in grotesque drunkenness (Venturi No.112, as a water-colour Venturi Nos. 820, 822, as a drawing Venturi Nos.1176–79, 1181) – a theme therefore which weighed very heavily on him.

The half-length portraits of these five years, all of friends of his youth in Aix (Venturi Nos.126–132), are psychologically fundamentally more differentiated than the spatulated portraits of 1865–67. Three large whole-length portraits of these years are however amongst the mightiest of all his creations: the portrait of the Aix painter 'Achille Emperaire' in an armchair (200 cm high by 122 cm broad; Venturi No.88), the portrait of his 'Father reading a Newspaper' in the same armchair (200 cm high by 120 cm broad; Venturi No.91) and the double portrait 'Paul Alexis reading to Zola' (131 cm high by 161 cm broad; Venturi No.117). It is difficult to say what is most remarkable about these portraits, their technical force, their boldness of composition or their human reality. If any of these three portraits were in the Louvre it would long ago have been placed on the same level as his contemporary Manet's pictures of people.

There are masterly works too amongst the still-life productions of these years, particularly 'The Black Grandfather-Clock' (Venturi No.69). What was still concealed in the bud in the still-life 'Loaf and Eggs' of 1865 has here blossomed abundantly – the rhythm of the three broad widths of white cloth hanging down at the bottom, the rhythm of the objects on the horizontals of the table in the middle (small cups to the right and in front of a large shell, small jars to the right and in front of a grandfather-clock) and finally the ending in repeated parallel verticals at the top. The colour is applied so thick that it may almost be caught in the hand and every figure is sharply defined, with the light coming in front of the dark; although it is still chiaroscuro painting in tones rather than colours, yet it offers the sharpest contrast to the plein-air dissolution and evanescence of form. Here form, as contour, surface and body, is already everything to Cézanne.

In the landscapes of these years too (Venturi Nos. 39–45, 47–58) the impenetrable spatula-built dark masses of the landscapes of 1865–67 break up. Occasionally Cézanne even experiments already with the shorter brush-stroke of the Impressionists (Venturi Nos. 39–41), and we even see occasionally the parallel rhythmical organisation of the brush-stroke which later becomes Cézanne's most characteristic signature (Venturi Nos. 47, 57). Most of the landscapes of this period are however painted with free strokes of the brush. Where streets or buildings are foreshortened, their perspective is deformed in the same way as the anatomy of bodies (Venturi Nos. 45, 49, 53, 54). On the whole the landscape, with few exceptions, was clearly more in the nature of an exercise than anything else. The two most important exceptions are the 'Melting of the Snows at Estaque' (Venturi No. 51) and the 'Railway Cutting' (Venturi No. 50). The 'Melting of the Snows' is, with its wild curves and its abrupt chiaroscuro, like some possible stage for a tempestuous scene with figures. The most masterly of all landscapes of the early period is however the famous 'Railway Cutting', as the 'Black Grandfather-Clock' is the most masterly still-life. This landscape too is already full of rhythm, horizontal rhythm of the walls in the foreground and the horizon behind, vertical rhythm of the two houses on the left and in the middle, and diagonal rhythm of the dark railway cutting in the middle and the Montagne Sainte-Victoire on the right. The man who fitted together the cuboid forms of this sublime picture is in his innermost nature opposed to all other painting of the nineteenth century.

When eventually Cézanne moved in 1872 to Pontoise where Pissarro was, he had naturally long known what 'Impressionism' was, even if the name was first coined on the occasion of the first Impressionist Exhibition in 1874. Equally he was aware that this new painting as good as negatived, technically and spiritually, nearly everything he himself had painted up to then. The decision to become a pupil of Pissarro presupposes therefore on the part of Cézanne a fundamental decision as to the meaning of art. Until now art had been for him subjective confession, an expression of the profound discord between him and the surrounding world, and the only artistic standard had been the sincerity and intensity of the expression.

Cézanne had produced under this banner works of the greatest power, which must have represented for him a great temptation to cling to this way as his own. Towards the end of the early period however he had been successful with works (the 'Black Grandfather-Clock' and the 'Railway Cutting') which he could not have regarded as less perfect, but which rested nevertheless on an entirely different conception of the meaning of art.

This new conception, which had clearly been at least dimly apprehended by Cézanne before his encounter with Impressionism is, however, not simply the antithesis of art as subjective confession, that is to say, art as objective recognition. Even in science there is no objective recognition, no recognition wholly divorced from the subject. And even thoroughgoing Naturalism, particularly its fundamental basis of space constructed by linear perspective, is by definition related to the subject. Even colour perspective and aerial perspective are realities only in the eye of the subject as spectator. Pleinairism is the complete avowal of the subjectivity (anyway physically conditioned) of our vision. And, when the Impressionists painted the brown shadows of Pleinairism blue, they did not claim that the shadows were blue but, correctly, only that they saw them as blue. That the blue shadows of the Impressionists were only their asses of Kish which they went forth to seek, whilst the triumph over plein-air prose and the foundation of painting on the harmony of pure colours were the kingdom into which they entered, these are other matters.

The idea which Cézanne must have already been carrying dimly in his mind when he first encountered Impressionism was the idea of an art which should neither lose itself in the subjective nor in the objective, nor yet be serenely resigned to our perceiving only a coloured shimmering light from things in the far distance, to there being therefore an unbridgeable gulf between subject and object. Cézanne's idea was rather that of an art which, without falling back into the trivialities of the old naturalism, should once more close with things and wrest from them the law of their form, knowing that there is an essential correspondence between the structure of things and the structure of our perception; the idea of an art, therefore, in which both poles of subjectivity and objectivity should be equally strong.

Cézanne must also have known beforehand that he would find in Impressionism, an art of warm, serene, relaxed abandonment to the beautiful coloured appearance of things, only release from his troubles of expression. As a physic however this must have been just right for him at the time.

Only thus, I believe, is the astonishing fact to be explained, that not one of Cézanne's so-called 'impressionist' pictures is in fact Impressionist, but that, on the contrary, the first picture he painted under the eyes of Pissarro was in its fundamentals completely opposed to Impressionism.

The only thing which Cézanne took over completely from Impressionism was the technical consequence of his overcoming of the melancholy preoccupation with self, and consisted in the complete banishment of absolute black and absolute white from his palette. The lighter grey and brown tones of late Pleinairism also very soon make way for the pure colours of the spectrum. The second important characteristic of Impressionism, the use of dots of colour, which was, for the Impressionists, closely bound up with the analysis of natural white light into the colours of the spectrum, was indeed adopted by Cézanne, but was immediately turned into its opposite.

Cézanne's first 'impressionist' picture, the famous 'Hanged Man's House at Auvers' (Venturi No.133) is for the most part painted with the spatula, built up like the portraits of Uncle Dominique; nevertheless it contains at bottom the whole mature Cézanne. Here already Cézanne has only one concern – the form and the inter-relationship of forms, or the rhythm. Here already what interested him in the object – wall, roof, chimney, tree – was only its basic form as expressed in geometric surfaces and stereometric volumes (the wall as a vertically dressed plane, the roof as a diagonally dressed plane, the chimney as a cube, the tree as a cylinder), and the rhythmical tension between these basic forms of objects.

Simple though this may sound in theory when we look back at it (and it expresses in a nutshell Cézanne's whole theory of art), yet the world of the pictures which had been opened to him by the key of this theory is inexhaustibly rich, though much hard work was still needed before the syntax of this new language became completely clear.

The 'Hanged Man's House' is characteristic of the whole mature Cézanne in another way. The title has nothing at all to do with works of the early period like 'Murder' and 'Strangulation', as the house was called by this name by the inhabitants of Auvers; nevertheless this picture has in its spiritual expression as well as in its melancholy subject an austerity and vehemence, in comparison with which the pictures of the Impressionists strike one as bohemianly carefree and light-weight. Cézanne had indeed by now overcome for ever the pessimism of his early period, but he was not able just to join in the Impressionists' chorus of rather childlike optimism. In all the paintings of the mature Cézanne it is as if there were an accompaniment of rolling thunder in the distance. The spiritual attitude of the whole of his mature period contains contradictions in sublime and almost mysterious fashion: the deepest gravity and the most cheerful lightheartedness, the most sublime spirituality and the most serene sensuality, the almost dogmatic emphasis of the legislator and the complete abandonment to the diversity of chance and fancy.

The division of the mature period into three parts as proposed by Venturi is in accordance with the facts, but must not be understood as if there were sudden complete changes such as existed between the early and mature periods. As Cézanne only dated few of his works himself and worked at some for years, the chronology of most of them can only be determined relatively. A work of the early Seventies is certainly clearly distinguishable from a work of the middle of the Eighties and one of the Eighties from a late work after 1900; but from one period to another there are only the gentlest of transitions, only gradual shifts. Another thing too makes it difficult to divide the three periods sharply from one another. Cézanne never completely abandoned an earlier achievement from one period to another; something which was later made clearer, or which later predominated, had always been there before in embryo. For that reason all the artistic media of the period of maturity must be discussed at its very beginning.

Let us take the most characteristic element of the 'impressionist period' (1872–77): the concise brush-stroke. Cézanne never indeed abandoned the spatula technique of the 'Hanged Man's House', and he often, particularly in the Eighties, built up in solid surfaces with the brush 'as if with a spatula'. Nevertheless Cézanne owes something very important to the Impressionist brush-stroke; not by taking it over just as it is, but by remodelling it to be his own characteristic signature. After the few pre-1870 experiments we find in 1873, for the first time, what we may call 'Impressionist brush-work'. Whilst however the short brush-strokes of the Impressionists are intentionally relaxed and free in direction, Cézanne's have right from the beginning an emphatic expression of direction, diagonal, vertical or horizontal. The individual stroke of the brush then increasingly becomes broader and thereby acquires a flat-pattern character; at the same time these directionally emphasised,

18 flat-pattern brush-strokes are repeated in parallel form. The brush-strokes with rhythm thus achieved in them are the germ cells from which the mature Cézanne achieves rhythm in the entire picture. The secret of the unique rhythmical richness of the mature Cézanne lies in the fact that not only is the general composition of a picture built up rhythmically, but the whole picture plane is impregnated with rhythms from every single brush-stroke, and, even in the most 'finished' painting, every brush-stroke remains visible as a stone in the building and shines forth in characteristic undistorted vivacity.

Whilst Impressionism, however, resolves every form – line, plane and volume – into dots of the brush, Cézanne is, even in his 'impressionist' period, aware not only of the flat brush-stroke but also of line, and of line in its double possibility: as contour delimiting surfaces and as independent form. The chief function of line lies in its direction in the picture plane: horizontal, vertical, diagonal and rounded. The interplay of the lines emphasising direction is, together with the rhythmical vitality of the brush-strokes, the most important element in the rhythmical organisation of the picture plane.

When a line delimits an object it creates a plane. Cézanne seeks passionately in the linear delimitation of objects their basic geometric two-dimensional form. Apart from the active line drawn to delimit a plane, that is to say, the line as contour, Cézanne recognises also an, as it were, passive line arising from the meeting of lighter and darker colour surfaces. The whole picture plane is filled with surfaces delimited by either active or passive linear means. In their form (rectangle, triangle, circle), in their size and in their disposition, the single planes are an additional element in the rhythmical construction of the picture.

The meeting of lighter and darker colour surfaces causes not only passive lines but, primarily, volume. Just as Cézanne looks in the linear delimitation of things for their basic geometric two-dimensional form, so also he looks in the delimitation of things as surfaces for their basic stereometric form as volume. We shall scarcely go wrong if we regard as the two most passionately pursued of Cézanne's aims the rhythmical construction of the picture and the fathoming of the basic form of things in line, plane and volume. In the late Seventies and the Eighties the passion for volume in its elementary form is so preponderant, that one is justified in speaking of this Cézanne as the 'cubist'.

Linear perspective, the second method (with chiaroscuro) of representing volume was known to Cézanne both in his early period and later, but as, by constant deformations, he robbed it of its decisive effect of creating the illusion of volume, there remained to him as a method of creating substantial form only colour contrast.

We come now to space. The question does indeed arise continually in Cézanne's pictures (in the early period too) in that we see streets, walls, houses or tables delimited by diagonally converging lines. But here too we miss the decisive characteristic without which the illusion of space is not created for our eye, namely the common vanishing-point, to which all these diagonal lines should lead. Therefore the lines of recession in Cézanne do not have spatial value, but only linear two-dimensional. A 'foreshortened' street or a 'foreshortened' table is a diagonally delimited trapezoid, a 'foreshortened' plate an oval (and usually a deformed one). The fact that Cézanne does not seek the spatial but, rather, avoids it, is revealed also in his predilection for views from above with the planes elongated downwards. This applies to most of his floors and tables.

The second method of creating the illusion of space, by colour perspective (warm colours forward, cold colours back), had already been weakened by the Impressionists because of their mixing with warm foreground colours their cold complementary colours, and with the cold background colours their warm complementary colours. As Cézanne took over from the Impressionists the principle of the contrast of complementaries and developed it further, he also does not use colour perspective. Often indeed he consciously places a cold colour in the foreground and a warm colour in the background, clearly with the set purpose of counteracting colour-perspective illusion of space.

Aerial perspective too (increased brightness and decreased sharpness of detail from front to rear) means as little to Cézanne as to Impressionism. It means nothing to Impressionism because for it foreground and background are equally bright and equally blurred, and to Cézanne because he distributes light and dark over the whole picture plane purely according to considerations of two-dimensional rhythms, and similarly with dissolving and sharply defined forms.

Finally, after line, plane, volume and space, we come to the last of the pictorial dimensions – time, that is to say the substance as it moves in space. Pleinairism was concerned with making movement directly visible and not merely representing it in statically fixed gestures, which was all that Classicism could do; it therefore blurred the linear outlines of things and thereby succeeded in really making the atmosphere shimmer, waves break, clouds scud across the sky and leaves flutter in the wind. Sharp outlines present the object in a single timeless moment; blurred outlines present it in a shorter or longer stretch of time. In this respect Impressionism is no more than the continuation of Pleinairism.

Since Cézanne makes the delimiting line so very significant once more, he again deprives things of their ability to move. This renunciation of movement is, for Cézanne, the expression of a fundamentally different spiritual attitude. Whilst Pleinairism and Impressionism are not concerned with the things themselves but with the changes of light in the space between and above things, with the change in the time of day, in the seasons and the weather, Cézanne looks not for what changes but for what remains, not for what is conditioned by time, but for what is free and timeless. In Cézanne's pictures there are no times of day and no seasons. It is not what takes place in the space between things that is important for him but only the law inherent in things themselves.

It is here that the most important reservation has to be made in the whole of the late period. The statics of things, caught in fixed lines, planes and cubes, is the chief characteristic of Cézanne's 'constructive' period. The 'static' Cézanne is the classical Cézanne, long the only one considered, and the first to have a great historical influence. From the middle of the Nineties on, however, line loses its leading position. With the line the delimited plane necessarily also decreases in importance, and it follows equally that solidity is at least diminished. Of Cézanne's methods of representation there remains the surface-forming brush-stroke. It is retained in the late period and indeed triumphantly brought to a position of predominating authority – predominating not sole. The late pictures of the 'Montagne Sainte-Victoire' shortly before and after 1900 for example consist almost exclusively of broad brush-surfaces. The gradual dissolution of the linear and substantial from the middle of the Nineties on may be traced particularly clearly in the water-colours.

Very closely allied to this change of attitude is a gradual alteration in the technique of the brush-stroke. To the 'constructive', static-cubic Cézanne of the Eighties belongs the heavy, impasto laying-on of colour. In this period Cézanne veritably models his rocks, houses, fruits, vessels. During this period, drawing, water-colour, oil-painting are three clearly distinct stages on the road to artistic realization. As early as the beginning of the Nineties however the paint is occasionally laid on more thinly and liquidly. The technique of the water-colour begins to overlap onto the technique of the oil-painting. Thin, liquid colour means transparent – pellucid and translucent – colour. Over a blue brush-surface, for instance, there slips, only partially superimposed, a green brush-surface. Where blue and green pervade each other a blue-green is formed from the underlying, lucent blue and the superimposed, pellucid green, with the blue and green not, however, mingling, but preserving their full separate existence, just as superimposed parts in an orchestra do not mingle, but merely permeate one another. From this permeation by colour there springs, with the use of a few basic colours, the more complete colour orchestration which gives to Cézanne's late period its brightness and its greatness.

Another point is that spaciousness is created by this superimposition of transparent brush-surfaces, – not the spaciousness frozen by linear perspective and subject to rational calculation, but a wavering coming forward and sinking back of the underlying and superimposed colour surfaces. Space without measurable distances, space wholly set free – like the space in which the sounds of music live.

A consequence of this is that we again have movement. As the brush-surfaces are no longer enclosed within fixed linear boundaries they shift about amongst one another and detach themselves from one another in constant irresolution of movement. That is why the thought of music always presents itself when we consider Cézanne's late works.

This is the late Cézanne, fading about 1912 into the restless, inter-penetrating colour surfaces of Orphism, as about 1908 the constructive Cézanne faded into Cubism.

From all this, finally, there emerges Cézanne's unique and magnificent method of building up a picture. He neither has, in the classical way, a finished picture in his mind, which he then executes just as a craftsman on the basis of cartoons and detailed sketches, nor is the motif (landscape, portrait or still-life) something finished in itself which he has to translate into painting, as it was for the Impressionists. To express it in an exaggerated form, the empty canvas is for Cézanne just as finished and just as unfinished as the completely painted canvas. Cézanne's work begins with the disturbance of the equilibrium of the empty planes by taking a line, let us say a horizontal, from the motif and placing it, for example, top right on the canvas; this is the first stage of 'incompletion' of the picture. Then he sets over against this horizontal a vertical (again taken from the motif) at the bottom left; the vertical and horizontal are in equilibrium and we have the first stage of 'completion' of the picture. Beginning again, a diagonal ascending from left to right gives the second stage of incompletion. A diagonal ascending in the contrary sense from right to left forms the second stage of completion. After many further stages the basic linear scaffolding of the motif, whether it be landscape, still-life or portrait, is firmly erected, a complicated structure of direction and counter-direction. The drawings of the period of maturity give, from as early as 1872 on, countless examples of such splendidly finished states, each of which contains within itself at the same time the possibility of a completely new beginning. One such new beginning might be the attaching of a colour, one of those characteristic brush-surfaces, to one of these lines, let us say at the bottom left. Then a second parallel brush-surface alongside amplifies this new state of disequilibrium, of incompletion. A brush-surface at top right restores the equilibrium. And now another new beginning, an entirely new adventure; the motif has something in it about a red roof of a house. This concentrated, fiery red calls for much cool green. The orange of dazzling walls calls for blue shadows, a large green melon for a small red apple. So the work progresses, always proceeding from the disturbing to the restoring of the equilibrium of forms and colours, always finished and unfinished at the same time.

We may also call the actual beginning the thesis, the disturbing impulse the antithesis and the restoring of equilibrium the synthesis. And every synthesis is at the same time the thesis for a new beginning. Thus the pictures of Cézanne are in a continual, never-ending state of growth; indeed they are the process of growth itself, just as nature is every moment an ending and a new beginning. In the unfinished state which Cézanne himself admitted in all his works there lies the guarantee of their inexhaustibly flowing vivacity.

At the same time, however, Cézanne's creative activity takes place in the light of a radiantly clear sensibility. Every work of his hand is not only something which has grown as if naturally, but it is also, and to the same degree, something formed by the intellect. The deep satisfaction which each work of Cézanne's affords us lies in the fact that we share as perceptibly in the natural process of growth as in the intellectual process of achieving form. In the water-colour the circumstance of growth and achievement of form is particularly clear; that is why we were able at the beginning to characterise the water-colour as the most sublime fulfilment of Cézanne's art.

This unexampled, exemplary devotion of Cézanne's to the creative artistic process in the period 1872–1906 is matched by the outward uneventfulness of his life in these thirty-four years.

In the autumn of 1872 Cézanne moved from Pontoise to live in Auvers nearby and found there in Doctor Gachet, who later also tended Van Gogh, his first buyer. Cézanne did not leave Auvers again until May 1874, so important had it become for him to be near Pissarro. In the spring of 1874 Cézanne joined with Pissarro, Sisley, Monet, Renoir and Degas in the famous First Impressionist Exhibition. In the words of Georges Rivière, Cézanne was 'the one most abused'. The 'Hanged Man's House' was, however, bought by Count Doria. Théodore Duret too, the first historian of the Impressionists, in his search for 'five-legged beasts' acquired pictures by Cézanne. From 1874 on Cézanne took up again his restless, stubborn round between Aix and Paris. In Paris too he changed studios often, as even finding a smell disagreeable could make impossible for him the contemplation he needed for every stroke of the brush. In 1875 – submission to the Salon and rejection; Victor Chocquet, a highly-placed customs official, bought his first Cézanne picture. In 1876 – submission to the Salon and rejection. Cézanne did not join in the Second Impressionist Exhibition of the same year, but sent seventeen pictures to the Third. He took no part in the Fourth of 1879 or in any of the later ones to the Seventh and last in 1882. He still tried however to get into the Salon, in vain again in 1878 and 1879. It was more desirable to him to find official recognition in the Salon than to be the most outlawed amongst the whole band of outlaws. In the spring of 1878 his father learned of the existence of the son Paul and reduced the monthly allowance to a hundred francs. In the summer of 1881 Cézanne got to know at Pissarro's home in Pontoise the latter's youngest pupil, Paul Gauguin. In Cézanne's lifetime Gauguin was the only considerable artist to be permanently influenced by Cézanne. In January 1882 Renoir visited him at L'Estaque. The Salon in 1882 at last accepted one of Cézanne's pictures, but rejected him again in 1884. In the years 1882 and 1883 he was much engaged in drawing up his will; though only forty-three he was tormented by thoughts of death. In the spring of 1886 Cézanne became estranged from Zola, who had been a friend of his youth in Aix, because he took as applying to himself the figure of the broken-down painter who hangs himself in his studio in Zola's novel 'L'Œuvre'. In April 1886 came the legalisation of his relationship with Hortense, and in October 1886 the death of his father. From this time on, exhibitions and sales are only important to Cézanne from the point of view of morale, but this remains as important as ever it was. In 1889 the 'Hanged Man's House' was accepted for the World Exhibition and in January 1890 he exhibited in Brussels with Sisley, Van Gogh and Segantini. During the same year he made his only journey abroad – with his wife and son into Western Switzerland. In the autumn of 1894 at Monet's house in Giverny he came to know Rodin, Clemenceau, Mirbeau and Geffroy. The number of these acquaintanceships might lead one to suppose that he led a real social life, but actually the attempts to come into contact with other people almost consistently turned out disastrously. His self-reliance, to which grievous injury had been done from childhood on, would not again be made whole. When Rodin, then in Giverney, extended his hand to Cézanne, the unexpected gesture moved him to tears as he thanked Rodin on his knees. His constant self-criticism and his proud certainty of himself drove him ever more deeply into solitude. For periods of years we know nothing of Cézanne's life except the bare externals. When in 1894 Caillebotte's collection of Impressionists and with it also two pictures by Cézanne reached the Luxembourg Gallery and when in the following year Vollard had a great success with fifty of Cézanne's pictures, it was far too late to change Cézanne's attitude towards the world around. In these years too the infirmities of age began to set in (Cézanne was diabetic). Not yet sixty he felt himself an old man – and was one too.

About the middle of the Nineties an important alteration took place in his personal life. He had withdrawn more and more from his contemporaries, but now it happened more and more that younger painters and writers would come to him in deep admiration. To be the paternal, enthusiastic friend of the young was for Cézanne balm on the oldest of wounds. He had, moreover, a very clear idea of his situation: 'I am less the painter of my generation than of yours', he wrote in 1896 to one of his young friends. And when young artists visited the hermit of Aix, his innermost gaiety would break through in his good hours. In 1901 Maurice Denis exhibited his largescale composition 'Homage to Cézanne', with Redon, Denis, Sérusier, Bonnard, Vuillard and others in an admiring circle around a still-life of Cézanne's. After 1902 his illness made rapid progress. His last visit to Paris was for the Salon d'Automne of 1904, which did him honour in a room to himself containing forty-two of his pictures. The ten pictures of the Salon d'Automne of 1906 were a mark of honour to a dying man; on the 22nd of October Cézanne, at the age of sixty-seven, succumbed to pneumonia brought about when he was surprised by a storm as he was painting the picture 'Cabanon de Jourdan'. Deeply affected by the great memorial exhibition in the Salon d'Automne of 1907, Picasso and Braque entered in 1908 into the creative heritage of Cézanne.

Let us notice finally that the change from the subjectivity of the early period to the objectivity of the period of maturity has as its consequence also a marked shift in the subjects of the pictures. Of the four themes characteristic for the whole of Cézanne – the composition with figures, the portrait, the landscape and the still-life – the first two are preponderant in the early period. In the period of maturity the emphasis shifts to landscape and still-life, themes which are already by their very nature more objective. Of about 800 oil-paintings in Venturi about 40 compositions with figures, 40 portraits, 30 landscapes and 15 still-life pictures come in the early 25 period before 1872, whilst the period of maturity after 1872 has about 130 compositions with figures, 100 portraits, 280 landscapes and 165 still-life pictures.

This purely quantitative shift is however quite materially accentuated by a changed spiritual attitude in the compositions with figures and in the portraits just after 1872.

It is true that we find amongst the compositions with figures between 1872 and 1877 the typical themes of erotic repression still occurring, and occasionally indeed the same idea for a picture as before 1872: 'Afternoon in Naples' (Venturi Nos. 223, 224), 'Modern Olympia' (Venturi No. 225), 'Temptation of Saint Anthony' (Venturi Nos. 240, 241),' The Eternal Feminine' (Venturi No. 247), 'Bathsheba' (Venturi Nos. 252, 253, 255), 'The Struggle of Love' (Venturi Nos. 379, 380). Even in the middle of the Eighties he is still painting a 'Judgement of Paris' (Venturi No. 537) and a 'Leda with Swan' (Venturi No. 550). But the mere facts of the brighter coloration and the lighter application of colour (both consequences of the contact with Impressionism) relieve these presentations of the melancholic expression of the Sixties. When one adds to this the anti-Impressionist achievement of rhythm by the parallelistic brushstrokes and by the linear stresses accentuating the form, these representations take on an almost bacchanalian dancing quality and vivacity (see Plate 4, of Venturi Nos. 379, 380). The little copy after Delacroix's 'Medea' of about 1880 (see Plate 2) is like a last farewell to the dark thoughts of the early period.

As had already occasionally occurred at the end of the Sixties there now appear more often alongside these distinctive subjects more neutral formulations: 'Conversation in the Open Air' (Venturi No. 231), 'Musical Group out of doors' (Venturi No. 234), 'Breakfast on the Grass' (Venturi Nos. 238, 377), the last of which falls in the beginning of the Eighties. Now however all these productions have an air of cheerful sociability (see Plate 3).

The compositions with figures attain complete neutralisation in the subject of the 'Bathers'. As early as 1873 we come across the earliest attempts at combining nude bodies, of women or men, which have no other function than to lie, to sit or to stand with meadow, water, tree, bushes or clouds in rhythmically constructed compositions. This expressively neutral form of figure composition then quickly becomes preponderant, and in the Eighties Cézanne succeeds in many versions in achieving the classical agreement between diagonal sitting and vertical standing.

Whilst however all these figure compositions of the Seventies and Eighties are

26   either of small size (up to 50 cm), or at most medium size (up to 100 cm), Cézanne
in the late period (1898–1905) three times magnified the theme of the 'Bathers' to
really mural proportions (the largest version, Venturi No. 719, measures 208 by 249
cm). In contrast to the static solutions of the Eighties (see Plate 5) these late versions
are full of a dynamic energy of diagonals mutually rising to a peak (see Plate 6).

In the portraits, too, the expressively psychological interest rapidly gives way after
1872 to the formal interest in the work as a picture. This is not to say that the human
interest in the subject is wholly lost, but it is no longer the interest in the blazoning
abroad of the personal confession as it was in the portraits before 1872. Even just
after 1872 we find Cézanne developing a more objective, and as it were indirect
method of representing people, which consists in forming the whole optical appearance of the subject into a picture using the purely pictorial media, line, surface,
volume and colour. Thus originate about 1877 the first classic self-portraits and the
first classic portraits of his wife. About a quarter of all the portraits of his mature
period are portraits of his wife; this in itself is convincing proof that the picture is
now more important for him than direct human assertion. As indirect assertion
however these portraits are by no means without human content.

  In second place, numbering about a fifth of all portraits of the period of maturity,
come the self-portraits. They too are at most involuntary and indirect personal
confessions. As such however they are very valuable. They are not the expression
of the mood of a moment but of a lasting spiritual attitude, of the spiritual attitude
of Cézanne during the whole period of his maturity. In all the self-portraits after
1872 he is concerned neither with confession nor with understanding himself, but
with understanding the object and understanding the picture; Cézanne is himself
just an object, and his only ends are the pictorial means. Cézanne, in the self-
portraits of the period of maturity, appears before us (see Plate 1) in utmost modesty
and objectivity, a scientist rather than an artist in the popular sense of a bohemian
genius. The famous portraits of Chocquet (Venturi No. 283), Geffroy (Venturi
No. 692) and Vollard (Venturi No. 696) show what a great measure of the essential nature of a subject Cézanne's indirect method can reveal.

  The culmination of the objective representation of people is achieved however in
the different versions of the 'Card-players' (1890–92, Venturi Nos. 556–60; cf.
Plate 30*). Although each figure is based on exact portrait studies and retains the

  * The figure does not occur in the painting 'The Card-players'; the table in the 1890-92 picture
is a simple inn table with straight under-edge; the water-colour's table with curved under-edge

individual traits of the portraits to the last detail, yet the whole far exceeds the portrait. The two main versions (Venturi Nos. 559, 560) are perhaps the most magnificent pictorial structures Cézanne ever built, and they are at the same time the clearest acknowledgements by the mature Cézanne of an unpretentious, objective humanity. In these pictures everything is made up of the most individual human expression and form coming together in one – every fold of a garment, every shape of a hat, every position of a hand, even the most fortuitous situation of a playing-card. The same applies to the slightly later series of the 'Smoker' (1895–1900, Venturi Nos. 684, 686, 688; cf. Plate 29).

The great picture of the 'Harlequin', for which his son, whom he loved above all else, had stood as a model (1888, Venturi No. 552; cf. Plate 28) has a notably expressive and even veiled confessional character. Once again, in the middle of the Nineties, Cézanne, in this shy, veiled way, sang a hymn to youth – in the different versions of the 'Boy in a Red Waistcoat' (Venturi Nos. 680–83; cf. Plate 31). And finally, in 1904–05, after he had painted his last self-portrait just before 1900, Cézanne sketched, with pitiless truth and using the freer media of the late period, the break-up of old age – in the portraits of the gardener Vallier (Venturi Nos. 715–18; cf. Plate 32).

His actual critical artistic interest during the whole of the period of maturity turns in good weather to the landscape, in bad to the still-life. In these two types of picture the whole formal power and formal wealth of Cézanne reveal themselves. It is impossible to name even the most masterly among the landscapes and still-life pictures of the period of maturity, let alone to describe them, as one would really have to do if one were to grasp the diversity of their formal and chromatic nature.

In the landscapes Cézanne discovered the law of the internal structure of the most contrasting types of landscape, of the hilly inland districts, the craggy coast, the cultivated park, the virgin wood, the village nestling between orchards, the towering mountain town of the South, the steeply cut quarry, the mountain rising bare and solitary. Here too all this understanding of the object comes only indirectly, not by Cézanne's copying the subject-matter, but by his building it anew in the picture with the elemental pictorial media of the painter. This has as its consequence that the onlooker experiences simultaneously the building of the picture and of the object.

only reappears in late still-life paintings – e.g. Venturi No. 730, 1895–1900; so perhaps not a 'Card-player' at all?

Our thirteen landscape water-colours (Plates 7–19) give at least some inkling of this richness; but we can see quite clearly in them the shift which occurs twice within the period of maturity. Plates 7 and 8 are still relatively near the impressionistic freer brush-stroke. Plate 8 is, in comparison with Plate 7, already stricter and finer in the horizontal-vertical-diagonal construction of the picture. Plate 9 grasps things more two-dimensionally and stresses more clearly their linear delimitation. Plates 10–14 show the constructive Cézanne in his full mastery. Plate 10: the lapidary antithesis of the vertical space at the left, of the straight horizontals of the railway-bridge and the wavy horizontals of the mountains at the right. Plate 11: the vertical of the trunk and the branches spreading out in multifarious diagonals. Plate 12: classical in the most sensitive placing of its basic form and colour stresses. Plate 13: behind the network of organically twining branches cubically constructed houses. Plate 14: the threefold contrast between rectilinearly designed human creation, luxuriant forms of growth of the bushes and the soft form of the mountain like some demolition. Plates 15–19 belong to the late period. The constructive law is no longer dogmatically accentuated but presupposed as something self-evident. Colour however triumphs in the most manifold permeations. Plates 17–19: the three famous motifs of the late period: Château Noir, Montagne Sainte-Victoire and Cabanon de Jourdan.

Finally in the still-life the interest of the subject-matter gives way in itself before formal interest. That is why Cézanne's still-life pictures are perhaps the most purely spiritual of all his works. Only seldom does Cézanne interest himself in the subjects as such. Usually the way they are brought together is entirely 'meaningless', for the whole meaning is usually in the bringing-together itself, that is to say in the rhythmical construction of the picture. The still-life is even as a motif a free creation of Cézanne's – how much more so then the finished picture! The 'basic subject' of Cézanne's still-life pictures is the round apple. There follow: the peach, melon, lemon, pear, loaf, plate, tumbler, wine-glass, bottle, jug, jar, table, tablecloth, curtain, wall, wall-paper and, again and again, the knife laid diagonally. The quickly fading flower, the favourite subject therefore of the Impressionist still-life, is less to Cézanne's taste. It is superfluous to add that Cézanne is not concerned with the material nature of his subject, but only with its form and colour.

Even just after 1872 we find most complete still-life pictures. It is only to be expected however that the constructive period should bring the culmination of the still-life. The still-life pictures of the late period often rise to an almost sublime richness. Our eight water-colours (Plates 20–27) begin only at the end of the Eighties. Plate 20: a hymn to the green growth of geranium leaves full of sap. Plate 21: the many, pointed leaves hanging down and the single, rounded vase standing upright. Plate 22: the ingeniously gathered folds of a heavy curtain. Plate 23: laid out horizontally a blue tumbler, yellow peach, yellow pear, green apple, and over them the single diagonal of the blue handle of the pan. Plate 24: self-denyingly severe, with on the left in an oval plate six apples, one in the middle, five round the edge of the plate, on the right an apple and a wine-glass, with above a vertically striped wallpaper. Plate 25: in the richer, softer colour permeations of the later period, a blue tumbler between a large green melon and a small red apple. Plate 26: in the expanding construction of the picture in the late period, with on a horizontal table eight yellow apples at the foot of a blue wine-bottle, four apples on an oval plate at the foot of a jug patterned in vivid colours, four apples at the foot of a blue jar – a knife laid diagonally. Plate 27: a skull lacking a lower jaw, forming part of the skull series of the late period (Venturi Nos. 751, 753, 758, 759) all having to the same extent and the same effect an expressive intention as have too the late Vallier portraits.

Dating of the pictures

For those pictures listed by Venturi his dating is adopted unless otherwise stated. For those not listed by Venturi a proposed dating is offered.

Colour Photographs

Basle, Hans Hinz: 4, 6, 8, 9, 11, 15, 16, 19, 22, 25, 27, 30. – New York, Francis G. Mayer, Art Color Slides, Inc.: 1, 5, 7, 17, 31, 32. – New York, Angelo Pinto, Photographic Illustrators, Inc.: 29. – Paris, Louis Laniepce: 3, 14, 20, 23, 24. – Vienna, Graphische Sammlung Albertina: 10.

PLATES

1

Self-Portrait

About 1894 – 26,3×21,9 cm.

Zurich, Walter Feilchenfeldt

Not in Venturi; study for Venturi painting No. 578, 1892–94

2

Medea (after Delacroix)

1879–82 – 39 × 26,5 cm.

Zurich, Kunsthaus

Venturi, No. 867

3

Musical Group out of doors

1872–77 – 12,9×14,5 cm.

Paris, Ph. Gangnat

Venturi, No. 875; study for Venturi painting No. 234, 1873–75

4

The Struggle of Love
1875–76 – 15×22 cm.
Zurich, Walter Feilchenfeldt
Venturi, No.897; study for Venturi painting Nos.379 and 380, 1875–76

5

Standing Bather

1879–82 – 21,3 × 15 cm.

Hartford, Conn., Wadsworth Atheneum

Venturi, No. 903; study for Venturi painting Nos. 389, 390, 393 and 394, 1879–82

6

Women bathing

1895–1900 – 17×26 cm.

Zurich, Emil Bührle

Venturi, No.1104

7

Landscape

Dated 1883–87 in Venturi, but more probably about 1877 – 36×30 cm.
New York, Wildenstein & Co.
Venturi, No. 972

8

Landscape near Pontoise

1879–82 – 31,5 × 49 cm.

Zurich, Walter Feilchenfeldt

Not in Venturi; cf. Venturi painting No. 319, 1879–82

9

Landscape near Marseille (Montagne Marseilleveyre)

1882–85 – 29×45,5 cm.

Zurich, Kunsthaus

Venturi, No.915; study for Venturi painting No.408,1882–85

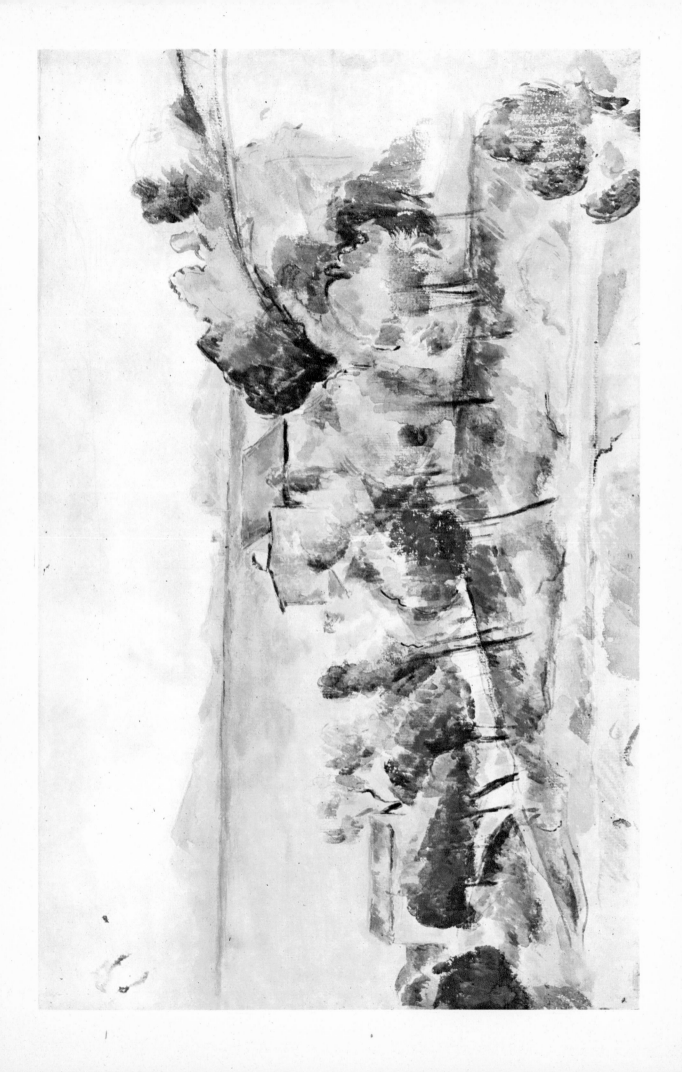

10

The Viaduct in the Valley of the Arc

1883–87 – 29,6×47 cm.

Vienna, Albertina

Venturi, No. 913; study for Venturi painting Nos. 452 and 453, 1885–87

11

Study for a Tree

1885–90 – 27×43,5 cm.

Zurich, Kunsthaus

Venturi, No. 1024

12

Provencal Landscape

1885–86 – 31,3 × 47,4 cm.

Lausanne, G. F. Reber

Venturi, No. 909; cf. Venturi painting No. 436, 1885–86

13

Trees and Houses

1883–87 – 32×46 cm.

Formerly Berlin, **Mrs.** Oppenheim

Venturi, No. 943; study for Venturi painting Nos. 479 and 480, 1885–87

14

Mill

1890–94 – 42×54 cm.

Paris, Musée du Louvre

Venturi, No. 979

15

The Bridge beneath the Trees

1894–98 – **46**×30 cm.

Zurich, Private Collection

Not in Venturi

16

Winding Road

About 1900 – 47×30,5 cm.

Basle, Robert von Hirsch

Not in Venturi; cf. Venturi water-colours Nos. 1555 and 1556, 1900-06

17

'Château Noir'

1900–1904 – 34,5×57,5 cm.

Chicago, Mrs. Potter Palmer

Venturi, No.1036; study for Venturi painting Nos.794 and 795, 1904–06

18

Montagne Sainte-Victoire

1900–1906 – 36×54 cm.

London, The Tate Gallery

Venturi, No. 1030; study for Venturi painting No. 803, 1905

19

The 'Cabanon de Jourdan'

1906 – 48×62,8 cm.

Ascona, Mrs. Bernhard Mayer

Venturi, No. 1078; study for Venturi painting No. 805, 1906

20

Geraniums

1888–90 – 31 × 27 cm.

Paris, Ph. Gangnat

Venturi, No. 1121

21

Leaves in a Green Vase

1885–95 – 48 × 31,3 cm.

Great Neck, L.I., Mr. and Mrs. Paul M. Hirschland

Venturi, No. 1117

22

Study of a Curtain

Dated 1890–1900 by Venturi, but more probably about 1890
Lausanne, Alfred Strölin
Venturi, No. 1124; study for Venturi painting No. 747, dated about 1900
by him, but more probably about 1890.

23

Fruit and Saucepan

1888–95 – **48**×28 cm.

Paris, Musée du Louvre

Venturi, No. 1540

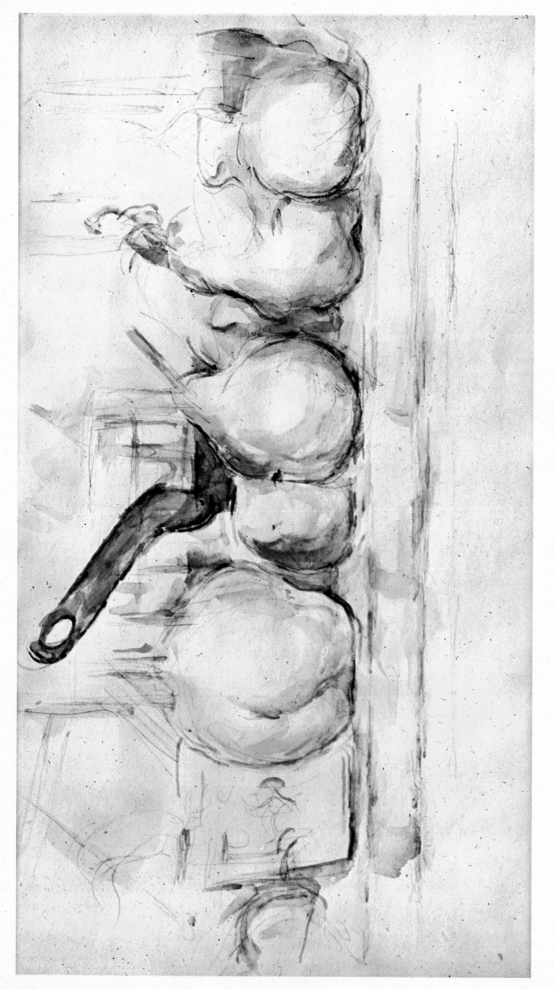

24

Apples and a Glass
1895–1900 – 20,5×26,5 cm.
Paris, Sacha Guitry
Venturi, No.1132; cf. Venturi painting No.742, 1895–1900

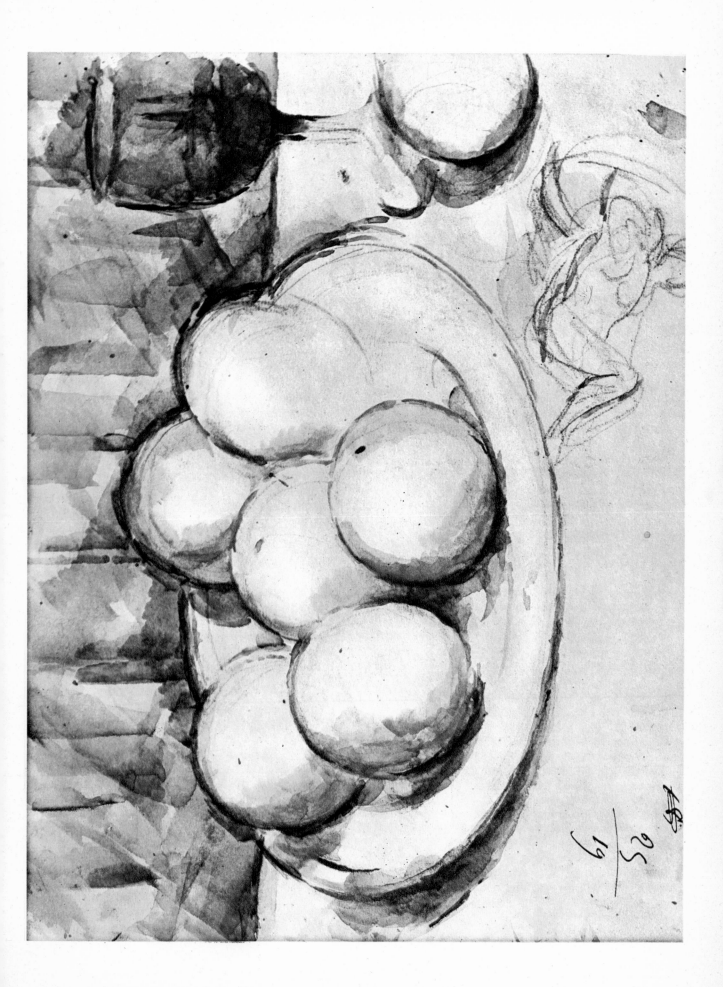

25

Still Life with Green Melon

About 1900 – 32×48 cm.

Basle, Robert von Hirsch

Not in Venturi

26

Apples on a Dresser

1900–06 – 48×62 cm.

New York, Private Collection

Venturi, No.1142; the brightly coloured jug is found frequently
in the late period: Venturi Nos.592,731,732,742,745

27

Skull

1895–1900 – 24,5×31,5 cm.

Winterthur, Georg Reinhart

Venturi, No.1130; cf. painting in Venturi Nos.751, 753, 758 and 759, 1895–1904

28

Harlequin

1888 – 50,5 × 23 cm.

Paris, Private Collection

Venturi, No. 1079; study for Venturi painting No. 552–555, 1888–90

29

The Smoker

1895–1900

Mevion, Pa., Barnes Foundation

Venturi No. 1087; study for Venturi painting Nos. 684 and 686, 1895–1900

30

Card-player

1895–1900 – 48,5 × 36,5 cm.

Basle, Robert von Hirsch

Venturi, No. 1099

31

Boy in a Red Waistcoat

1890–95 – 46,1×30,1 cm.

Zurich, Walter Feilchenfeldt

Venturi, No.1094; study for Venturi painting No.683, 1890–95

32

Portrait of Vallier

1906 – 48×32 cm.

Bradford, Pa., T. E. Hanley

Venturi, No. 1102; study for Venturi painting No. 718, 1906